Get
your juices
flowing!

Get
your juices flowing!

Table Of Contents

Foreword

Whether it is just a fad or an exercise that is here to stay, juicing is becoming more and more popular, especially for those who are very health conscious. However in order to get the best benefits out of the juicing exercise some points should be taken into careful consideration. Get all the info you need here.

Get Juiced!

Juicing your way to better health

Chapter 1:

Synopsis

Juicing can be incorporated into the daily lifestyle for the purpose of enhancing healthy living and it is also a good way on increasing the daily intake of fruits and vegetables.

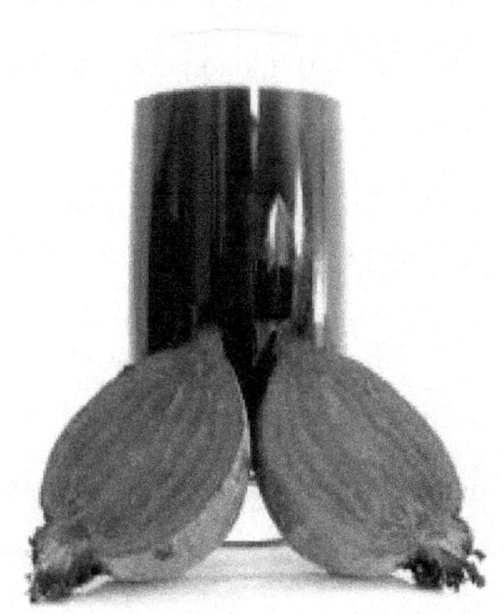

The Basics

For most people though juicing is either a chore and a bother or a welcomed alternative, however for those who enjoy juicing it is greatly encouraged as its better to do it personally than to buy juice products.

All juice products have to be treated and processed to ensure its integrity and shelf life, therefore homemade juices are a better choice to make.

However when doing homemade juices, it should be noted that it is very important to consume the juice product as soon as it is ready as letting it sit will only encourage the growth of pathogens and they also tend to break down faster when exposed to air, thus effectively losing a lot of its originally touted value.

It should also be noted that although consuming juices as a regular habit, limiting the juicing to only fresh fruits would not be a very good idea as a lot of fruits have a naturally high sugar content and are not so high in fiber, thus causing the negative build up of sugar levers in the body system. This may lead to diabetic and weight gain issues. A better alternative would be to combine complimenting fruits and vegetables together to form one delicious concoction that is both tasty and healthy. Accompanying this with a healthy fat and lean protein diet is also an added advantage.

Chapter 2:

Synopsis

As more people indulge in this form of healthy nutritional intake, it is becoming more popular to consume fruits and vegetable through juicing rather than eating these items as a whole and in its original form.

However scientist and nutritionist are or two minds when it comes to the merits of juicing as opposed to consuming these items whole, although there is yet to be any proven data to merit or advocate either choice over the other.

Advantages

There should however be some knowledge on the matter, before actually making juicing a permanent feature in an individual's lifestyle.

Studies have shown that juicing is one way of getting all the fruits and vegetable requirements into the body system effectively though albeit without the positive addition of the fiber needs.

It is arguably a more effective way of getting the nutrients adsorbed into the body system without putting undue pressure on the digestive system to break down the fibers.

For those who naturally have a dislike for consuming fruits and vegetable, juicing may present a more acceptable alternative.

There are also a variety of recopies available to make the juicing concoctions more agreeable and even tasty. Juicing combinations of vegetables and fruits are good to include in the recipe sourcing exercise.

Most juicing recipes include the parts of the fruits that would otherwise be discarded in the more conventional way of consuming them.

However with juicing the inclusion of pits, peelings, seeds and other parts are usually all included in the process for it has been noted that these contain a rich source of vital nutrients which are usually systematically thrown out.

Processed juices usually require some heating process to enhance the shelf life of the product and this can cause the enzymes to be killed. However with juicing this can be avoided and the enzyme content can be kept intact.

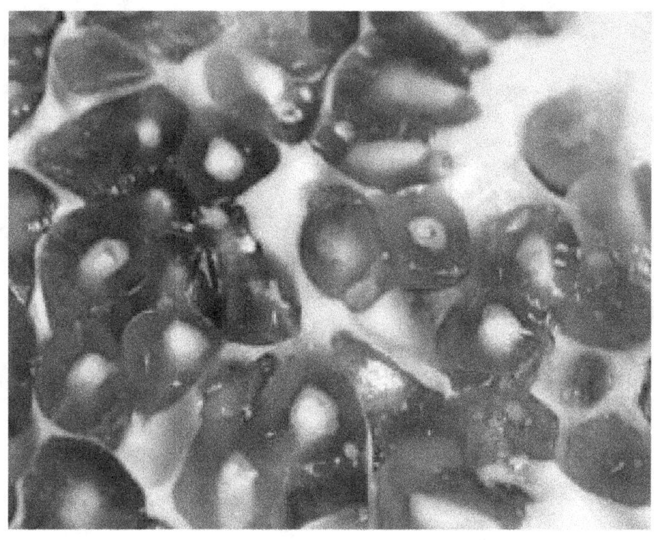

Chapter 3:

Healthy Juice Recipes

Synopsis

There are a lot of positive reason that eventually encourage more people to juicing and this may include the ability to save cash due to the fact that the fruits can be bought in bulk, the definite benefits it can bring to controlling weight gain and shrinking the waist line, creating a fulfilling and healthy diet plan and increasing the energy and vitality levels in an individual.

Recipes

The following are some of the more popular juice recipes for the avid juicer:

Lemony apple – 2 apples, 1 lemon, 1" slice of ginger. This is a healthy remedy for colds as it is rich in flavonoid content. It also has a fresh and tangy taste that is quite invigorating.

Plain O'O.J – 4 medium sized oranges. Remembering to include as much of the white membranes as possible is a good idea as this too is rich in bio-flavonoid. However in this case it would be a good idea to avoid including the whole peel as it might enhance the sour and raw taste, thus causing the juice to take on a rather unpleasant taste.

Alkaline juice – 1 cup of spinach, ½ cup of cucumber, 2 stalks of celery including the leaves. 3 carrots and ½ an apple. The skin of the dark green cucumber will provide the source of chlorophyll which is a phytochemical that can help to build up the red blood cells. The cucumbers also contain silica which is a mineral that is good for the skin.

A Very Berry Medley – 2 cups of strawberries, 2 cups of blueberries and 1.5 cups of raspberries. Berries are a popular choice for juicing due to its quick and easy breakdown process and its simple rinse action. Being a great source of antioxidants such as anthocyanins, flavonoid and ellagic acid all or which have good anti cancer and anti heart diseases benefits.

Pomegranate juice – 5 pomegranates. In this recipe only the seeds are used and the rest of the fruit is discarded. However some may find better results using a blender as the seed does present a challenge to break down.

Chapter 4:

Synopsis

Incorporating the juicing exercise into a weight loss diet plan is a very effective way to shed the weight. However it should be noted that the juicing process should ideally include both vegetables and fruits as concentrating on only fruits will not be beneficial because most fruits usually have high sugar contents.

Get The Fat Out

Juicing is also a good ingredient for any detoxifying exercise and it can be used as a meal replacement or when there is a fasting plan in place. If the juicing purpose is meant to detoxify, then it will function to push out all the toxins and fats that have accumulated over time in the body system.

These juices will work as cleansing agents which would be an ideal substitute to a heavy unhealthy meal. Juicing will also be a more healthy and realistic way to lose weight.

Most juicing recipes that are designed for weight loss are very nutritious and satisfying to ensure the individual does not have to resort to supplementing it with other food items due to hunger pangs.

They also usually include ingredients that are specifically part of the combination for the characteristics of sweeping away the toxins and fats.

It is also recommended to ensure that all the ingredients used in the juicing recipes are fresh produce and it should all be cleaned thoroughly before actually commencing the juicing exercise.

The following are some recopies that would serve well in the quest to juicing the fat away:

Apple berry fiber – the apples are excellent cleansing agents while the berries provide the mineral supplements.

Green pineapple – this concoction is simply refreshing and bursting with goodness and also feels very filling.

Orange pineapple chilli – being full of vitamin C, and having enzymes that can dissolve mucus accumulated in the body, it also speeds up the metabolic system.

Gingered pear – a great laxative option and good for digestion.

Chapter 5:

Juicing For Kids

Synopsis

Most times it is a struggle for both parents and children when it comes to tackling the issue of eating vegetables and fruits served at meals. However with the discovery of juicing this problem for most has been eradicated or at the very least decreased to controllable levels.

For The Little Ones

Juicing is a great and fun way to get nutrition into the bodies of growing children to ensure optimal development of their bodies. The trick is to design concoctions that are pleasant to drink and are also refreshing especially after a strenuous playing session.

However for younger children it would be advisable to dilute the juices, as the concentrated form may be too much for the underdeveloped body to deal with.

Teenagers and older kids should have to problems with drinking concentrated juices. Introducing juices to kids should be done in a gradual process with initial stages of diluting.

Choosing fruits that have delectable tastes is much better and less likely to be rejected by the child. Starting out with single juice choices before moving on the combinations is also advised, as this will allow the body system and the child's palate to get used to this introduction into the healthy daily diet plan.

Changing the juices and providing a variety is definitely an attractive feature for children and they would be fascinated with the colors and tastes reflected in the variety.

Once the favorite juices are identified, serving them as often as possible without boring the child will be beneficial. Using the favorite juice as a base, it may also be possible to add on a little portion of other fruits or vegetables to further enhance the nutrient content of the juice.

Some popular choices may include apple juice, pineapple and carrot juice, orange juice, orange and carrot juice pear juice and apple and grape juice.

Chapter 6:

Juicing For Anti-aging

Synopsis

Juicing is not the new fad to combat natural aging processes. If makes sense to opt for this healthier and cheaper yet no less effective way of starving off the aging process.

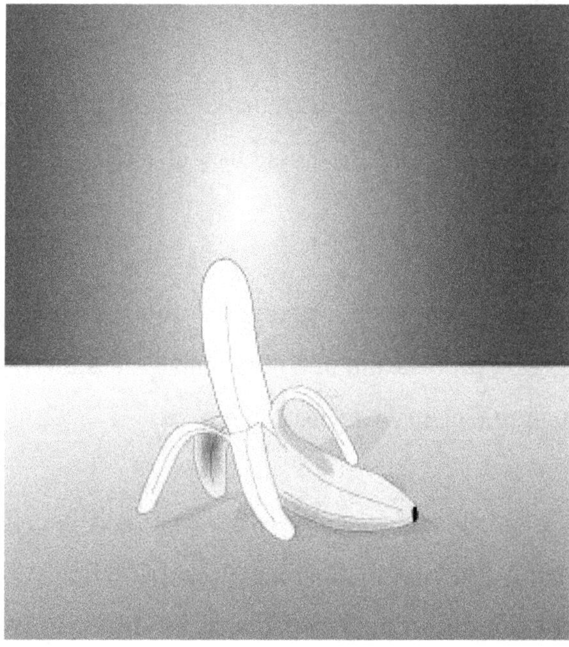

Staying Younger

Juicing benefits the body as it provides the combination of all the essential vitamins, minerals, amino acids, essential fatty acids, and enzymes.

These fruits and vegetable that are usually used in the juicing process are also power packed with anti aging and life preserving elements, thus the choice made to incorporate regular juicing exercises would benefit greatly.

The antioxidants and substances that neutralize the free radicals in the system ideally provide the possibility of having good anti aging benefits.

A diet rich with vitamins and minerals is the key factor to fighting against the aging process and one of the most pleasant ways of doing this is through the juicing exercise.

Brightly colored fruits and vegetables are especially beneficial for the anti aging fight. Fruits such as oranges, cherries, tangerines, apples, blueberries, cranberries, melons, bananas, grapes, berries, kiwi, and mangoes are all know for the anti aging properties.

These can be taken in combinations or separately, whichever is suitable for the individual's palate. When it comes to vegetable there is the abundant choice of carrots, squash, red and green cabbages, broccoli, spinach which are just as beneficial for their anti aging properties too.

Apple carrot detox – 1 apple, 1 slice of ginger, 1 carrot, ½ cup or water. Its excellent properties that creates healthy skin and eliminates toxin form the body is the reason this juice is a popular choice for many.

Cholesterol burner – 1 apple, ½ cucumber, 4 stalks of celery, ½ cup of water. This juice is a good controller of high cholesterol levels in the body system and also helps to fight against upset stomachs, besides the more obvious anti aging properties it carries.

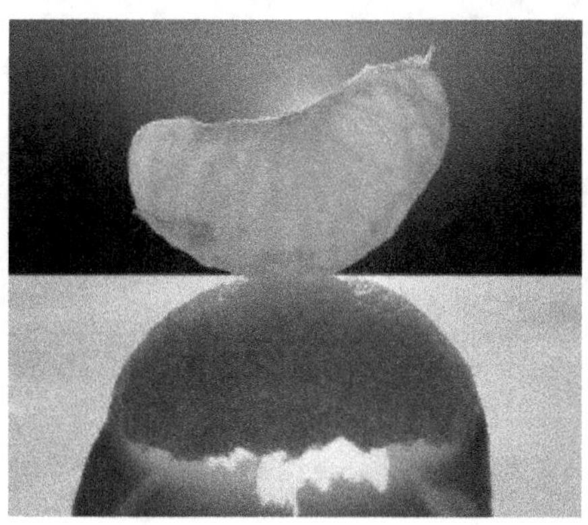

Chapter 7:

Synopsis

The juicing process is ideal for detoxification of the body system, as it enhances the enzymes, vitamins and mineral absorption which in turn greatly benefits the immune system.

Detox

Juicing organic vegetables and fruits which are rich in nutrients will help to cover the cells in the body with the alkaline juices released from these juicing concoctions whereby acids are released and toxins can be removed through various elimination channels in the body.

The parts of the body that play an important role in filtering such toxins would include the lungs, kidneys, skin and other functions like urinary and bowel movements.

The enzymes released from these juices also help the digestive processed where the proteins break down the foods into nutrients and this is an important function as most adults have already used up their natural digestive enzymes by the age of 30.

Therefore the outside aid that the juices provide is definitely beneficial to the digestive process as it is pivotal in the detoxifying regiment the body naturally enlists.

When the body is full of toxins it is unable to absorb the nutrients that are available in the natural intake of regular foods, thus the need for these added juices to assist in the breakdown of the toxins to cleanse the body and carry the appropriate amount to oxygen and nutrients directly to the cell and tissues.

Some of the ideal ingredients to use in the juicing process for detoxifying would include lettuce, dark green kale, carrots, beet greens, cilantro, parsley, celery sticks, collard greens, endive, spinach, dandelion greens, cabbage both purple and green and lemons.

Some people who practice this detoxifying regiment periodically attest to the fact that they no longer have cravings for sweetened foods and they can keep to a regular and healthy diet without any struggles. This is probably due to the fact that the body is able to function at its optimum because of the detoxifying sessions.

Chapter 8:

Social Marketing

Synopsis

It has already been established that juicing is a very healthy exercise to practice. This is also one of the contributing factors that ensure the individual's chances of developing any medical problems are considerably lessened. By lowering the risk of having diseases the juicing habit has proven to be one that everyone should consider for its merits.

Staying Healthy

There are several very specific combinations that can be used regularly of create the ideal effects within the body system that allow it to resist any possible occurrences of diseases.

One of which, is drinking a beetroot combination, as this is said to dramatically reduce the risks of heart disease, strokes, Alzheimer's and dementia.

The bright red juice contains the chemical nitrate which dramatically reduces blood pressure for almost everyone taking this remedy.

Another juice combination is the one with pomegranate content which is pivotal in lowering cardiovascular risks, however this should be taken with care as the potassium content is rather high. Tomato juice combinations are also supposed to help lower heart diseases and control diabetic symptoms.

Other benefits from consuming tomato juice would include the resistance to developing chronic diseases like cancer and coronary heart disease. This can be avoided because of the carotenoid content called lycopene which is richly found in tomatoes.

Some of the ingredients that can be used to combat or at least lower the risks of diseases would include broccoli, Brussels sprouts, butter squash, cabbage, Chinese broccoli, kale, spinach, parsley, collards greens, mustards green, chard, beetroot, carrots, cauliflower, cucumber, green pepper, sweet potatoes, lettuce and celery.

Regular combinations of these juices will help to keep the chemical balance in the body system which in turn will allow the body to perform at its prime thus effectively avoiding any diseases.

Chapter 9:
Juicing For Stress Relieving

Synopsis

Almost everyone adult and child alike has experienced bouts of stress at various points in their daily life. For most, this is taken in stride until it is no longer possible to do so, and when this happens it almost always affects the health conditions.

Destress

Fruit and vegetable juices have long been known for their stress relief and relaxation properties. Therefore taking the time to explore this healthy alternative to popping pill to relieve stress is certainly worth the effort.

Apple, cherry and blueberry ingredients have been known to be good health boosting elements where the flavonoid can facilitate better lung functions and with this optimum breathing position the ideal amounts of oxygen is then able to be circulated well with the body system thus relieving any internal pressures felt when stress levels are high and this eventually helps to lower the stress levels.

These ingredients can also contribute to relaxing the arteries and lowering the risk of cardiovascular diseases which are often caused by stress. Smoothies made from bananas, strawberry, peppermint and lemon can all help to relieve stress and create the relaxing overall body feeling.

When the adrenaline levels increase the body requires more vitamin C and as this cannot be naturally conjured by the human body there is a need to have this supplemented for outside sources, thus the advantage of the afore mentioned ingredients.

Bananas would contribute to stress relief properties while the peppermint which contains menthol will have a cooling effect on the body while the others will help in digestion, thus creating an overall effect that will combat any significant presence of stress.

Wrapping Up

New discoveries have shown consuming fruits and vegetables, in the form of juices have been able to show significant benefits to the body system when ingested in regular intervals.